Brownie Annual 2004

Stay safe

You should be able to have a go at everything in your great *Brownie Annual 2004*, but sometimes it's wise to ask an adult you know for help. You can still do it by yourself, just make sure the adult says it's OK and is watching.

Safety symbol

On some pages you'll see this symbol, to remind you that you might need a bit of help with the activity. If there isn't a symbol but you're still not sure, ask for help anyway.

Be safe

My Brownie web safe code

When using the world wide web I promise:

- ❀ to agree rules with my parents or guardians about the best way for me to use the computer and the world wide web.

- ❀ not to give out my home address or phone number without permission.

- ❀ not to give out the name or address of my school without permission.

- ❀ not to agree to meet anyone who I contact on the web, unless my parents or guardians say it is all right and go with me.

- ❀ not to put my photograph onto a web site.

- ❀ to tell my parents, guardians, teacher or Guider if I find something on the web that worries or upsets me.

Web safe

With thanks to the Girl Scouts of the USA for the ideas contained within this warning for children.

Brownie fun

Being a Brownie is a fantastic adventure. Brownies are always doing exciting activities. It's great fun being a Brownie!

Brownie Promise

I promise that I will do my best:
To love my God,
To serve the Queen and my country,
To help other people
and
To keep the Brownie Guide Law.

Brownie Law

A Brownie Guide thinks of others before herself and does a Good Turn every day.

Badge link

On most pages of this great *Brownie Annual 2004* there's a badge link box. The badges show that the ideas and activities on that page link to a Brownie badge. If you want to find out what you need to do to get the badge, look it up in the *Brownie Badge Book*. Remember when you do a badge, always do your best.

My special Brownie saying

Lend A Hand

Girlguiding UK

Contents

16 Brain-teasers
Puzzles with a leap year theme.

8 Planet piñata
A great idea for parties.

18 Going for gold
Get set for the Olympic games.

20 Food for all seasons
Yummy recipes all year round!

10 Bear necessities
Enter the wintry world of polar bears.

22 Super Brownie
Super Brownie visits the Guides...

12 Fab flowers
A flowery hair band to make.

26 Testing time
A fun experiment to try.

14 This is the key
A poem about an unusual kingdom.

28 Super science
Find out what scientists really do.

30 Photo tree
An unusual way to show off your photos.

32 Puzzle planet
Be a star – try these space puzzles.

34 Happy birthday Brownies!
Brownies are 90 years old!

The Brownie Guides who appear in this Annual are from 11th Battersea Park Brownie Pack and 1st and 2nd Pilgrims Hatch Brownie Packs.

Special thanks to: Terri Frame; Katie Walsh and Chloe Sheppard at Planet Science; Cadbury Trebor Bassett; missdorothy.com Ltd.; Lauren Goddard; Amanda Bailey at the RSPCA; Colwyn Griffiths; Pam Grimes and Sandy Sturman; Robert Strange.

Written by Alison Smith apart from: *Planet pinata* and *Bear necessities* by Elizabeth Duffey; *Super Brownie and the Guide Meeting* by Marion Thompson; *Miss Dorothy* by Wendy Watts and Alice Forbes.

Cover photograph by Laura Cartwright, Brownie photographs by Laura Cartwright

Brownie Annual 2004: An official publication of Girlguiding UK.
© The Guide Association 2003

All Brownie photographs © The Guide Association; all other photographs © as acknowledged on appropriate pages.

'Madame Giraffe' from JIM-JAM PYJAMAS by Gina Wilson published by Jonathan Cape. Used by permission of The Random House Group Limited.

Published by Girlguiding UK
17-19 Buckingham Palace Road
London SW1W 0PT
Web site www.girlguiding.org.uk

Girlguiding UK is an operating name of The Guide Association. Registered charity number 306016. Incorporated by Royal Charter.

Girlguiding UK Trading Service ordering code 6005
ISBN 0 85260 190 5

Patron HM The Queen
President HRH The Countess of Wessex
Chief Guide Jenny Leach
Brownie Adviser Sandra Moffitt
Project Editor Alison Smith
Design Team Jade Garner, Sarah Melrose, Heather Peters, Alexandra Valy
Cover Design Sarah Melrose
Production Les Girling
Colour repro InTouch Group plc
Printed and bound by Scotprint

Girlguiding UK

36 Cosmic cooking
Recipes that are out of this world!

38 The Bird of the Golden Land
A fairy tale starring a very clever horse...

42 Miss Dorothy
Have a go at Dot's safety quiz.

44 Funky monkeys
Monkey around with these fascinating animals.

46 Looking up
Make a handy periscope.

48 Competition
Win your Pack a trip to a sea life centre!

50 Mind-bogglers
Try these hot and cold puzzles.

52 Portugal
How much do you know about this country?

54 Greek treats
Delicious Greek dishes to make.

56 Madame Giraffe
A great animal poem.

58 Perfect pets
Learn how to care for gerbils.

60 Riding high
Find out about a popular sport.

62 Feathered friends
A beautiful mobile to make.

64 Best buddies
A Brownie Buddy photostory.

68 Brownie twisters
Tricky puzzles about Brownie traditions.

70 Time out
Fun facts about time and space.

72 Olympic feasts
Tasty treats with an Olympic theme.

74 Photo fun
Handy hints for taking great photos.

76 Answers
How well did you do at the puzzles?

Planet piñata

Children in Mexico celebrate their birthdays by playing piñata. They make a large, papier mâché shell which is filled with sweets and hung from the ceiling. The aim of the game is to break the piñata using a long stick. The catch is, you're blindfolded! Have a go at creating your own.

You need

2 newspapers ★ flour ★ warm water ★ large bowl ★ round balloon ★ pin ★ scissors ★ small wrapped sweets ★ paints and brushes ★ PVA glue ★ needle and strong thread

1

Tear one of the newspapers into strips about 2cm wide and 10cm long. Mix up some paste by stirring together a cup of flour with half a cup of warm water. It should be about as thick as glue. Put the paste in a large bowl.

Illustrated by Andi Good

2

Blow up the balloon until it is about the size of a football. Pull one of the newspaper strips through the paste, covering both sides. Lay the pasted strip over the balloon. Keep pasting until the balloon is completely covered. Make up more paste as you need it.

Leave the balloon to dry between each layer, then cover it with another layer of paper. Keep going until you have put on six layers of paper.

4

Stick a pin in to pop the balloon. Cut a small hole at the bottom of the ball and pull out the balloon. Fill the piñata with lots of sweets. Paste over the open hole with some more paper.

Paint the balloon to look like a planet. It could look like one of the planets in our solar system, or you could invent your own ideal world. When the paint is dry, cover it with a coat of PVA glue mixed with warm water.

Use a needle and thread to string up your piñata. Now it's ready for you to break — and catch all those sweets!

5

6

Fiesta facts

The first piñatas were used in Italy, but the idea travelled to Spain and then to Mexico.

Piñatas are also popular around Christmas time.

The person who breaks the piñata will have a year's good luck!

Bear necessities

Find out all about beautiful polar bears.

Wintry world

Polar bears live at the very top of the world, in the frozen far north of the Arctic Circle. They are very well adapted for the cold conditions. Their thick fur keeps them warm and its white colour helps them blend in with the snow. Their feet have padded soles that grip on the slippery ice.

Big bears

Polar bears are the largest carnivores (meat-eaters) in the world. Male bears are much larger than females. An average male bear weighs as much as six human adults. A really big one can stand up to three metres high.

Gentle giants?

Although they look cute and cuddly, polar bears can be dangerous. However, bears usually only come near humans when they can't find enough to eat. Very few people are injured by polar bears. Coming into contact with people is dangerous for the bears too, as they might be killed by hunters or poisoned by pollution.

NHPA/Andy Rouse

Cute cubs

Polar bear cubs are born in the winter and spend their first few months tucked safely in an underground den with their mother. Cubs will stay with their mother for about two years. During this time, she will teach her cubs how to hunt and look after themselves. They learn hunting and fighting skills through playing.

Bear town

Churchill in Canada is known as the polar bear capital of the world. Each year, many bears travel to the town where they wait for the sea to freeze. In Churchill there's a special polar bear 'jail'. Any bears that wander into the town are tranquillised and kept in the jail. They are then airlifted back out on to the ice, well away from the dangers of the human world.

NHPA/Andy Rouse

NHPA/Brian Hawkes

Get the facts

Native people of the Arctic have many names for polar bears. Lapps call them 'the old man in the fur cloak' and the Ket people of Siberia call them 'grandfather'.

Polar bears can sprint at up to 30 miles per hour, but they don't run for long as their heavy fur makes them too hot.

Polar bear cubs are as small as rats when they are born.

A polar bear has an amazing sense of smell. It could smell you from about 20 miles away!

Even though they're so big, polar bears are great tree climbers.

NHPA/Paal Hermansen

Feeding time

Polar bears eat mainly seals, which they hunt on the sea ice. A bear will sit quietly next to a hole in the ice, waiting for a seal to come up for air. When there isn't much food around the bears survive on blubber. This is a thick layer of fat under the bear's skin, which helps keep it warm as well as being an emergency food store.

Super swimmers

Polar bears are excellent swimmers. When they swim, the bears paddle with their strong front legs, using their back legs to steer. Their long fur is waterproof and also traps air, which helps them to float. Some sailors have seen bears as far as 60 miles out to sea. Living on their fat reserves, bears can swim for days at a time.

Fab flowers

This pretty flowery hair band is so easy to make. Choose felt and ribbon in colours to match your favourite outfit.

You need

pencil ★ paper ★ scissors ★ 2 pieces of felt in different colours ★ 70cm of thin ribbon ★ needle with a large eye

1

Draw a simple flower shape, about 3cm wide, on to the paper. Cut it out.

2

Lay the flower shape on to one piece of felt. Draw round it three times and cut out the flowers.

3 Draw a larger flower shape, about 4 ½cm across, on the paper. Cut it out. Place this on to the second piece of felt. Draw round it and cut it out.

4 Thread the needle on to the thin ribbon. Sew up through the centre of one of the small flowers. If you wiggle the needle around it will make a big enough hole for the ribbon to go through. Sew back down again to make a small stitch. This will be the centre of the flower.

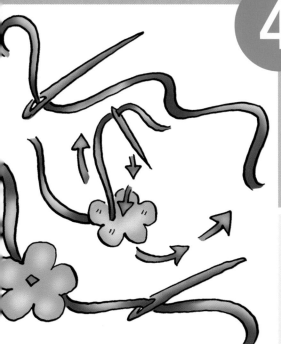

Lay another small flower on top of the large flower. Sew up through them both together, then down again.

Finally, sew on the last small flower in the same way as the first. Slide the flowers along the ribbon so the big one is in the middle. Slide the two small flowers into position.

5

6

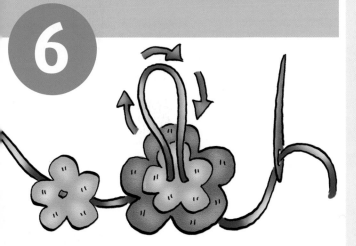

To put on your beautiful hair band, ask an adult to tie the ribbon around your hair. Hold it in place with hair grips.

This is the key

This is the key of the kingdom:
In that kingdom there is a city.
In that city there is a town.
In that town there is a street.
In that street there is a lane.
In that lane there is a yard.
In that yard there is a house.
In that house there is a room.
In that room there is a bed.
On that bed there is a basket.
In that basket there are some flowers.

Flowers in a basket.
Basket on the bed.
Bed in the room.
Room in the house.
House in the yard.
Yard in the lane.
Lane in the street.
Street in the town.
Town in the city.
City in the kingdom.
Of the kingdom this is the key.

Anon.

Illustrated by Claire Chrystall

Brain-teasers

Have a go at these fun puzzles around the theme of leap years.

Did you know?

The year 2004 is a leap year. This means that it has one extra day. In non-leap years there are 28 days in February, but in a leap year there are 29. A leap year happens every four years. So if you are born on February 29th, you only have a birthday once every four years!

Birthday girls

Follow the trails to match each girl to her birthday. Who was born in a leap year?

Many months

One month does not appear in the word search. Which one?

January
February
March
April
May
June
July
August
September
October
November
December

Y	S	J	B	B	U	F	H	M
R	D	E	M	N	S	C	A	M
A	E	C	A	P	R	I	L	Y
U	C	B	Y	A	R	A	S	T
R	E	B	M	E	T	P	E	S
B	M	N	Y	E	F	G	R	U
E	B	E	U	L	V	N	R	G
F	E	R	U	J	U	O	I	U
Y	R	A	U	N	A	J	N	A

Lost property

Nicki has lost her diary. Can you help her get through the maze to find it?

Illustrated by Phil Dobson

Check your calendars

Can you find ten differences between these two calendars?

All ages

Use the clues to work out in which year each girl was born.

1993   1994   1995   1996   1997

'I was born in a leap year.'

'I'm two years younger than Emma.'

Aimee

Joanne

'I'm older than Melissa.'

Emma

'I'm younger than Joanne.'

Ashleigh

Melissa

'I'm the second oldest.'

Different diaries

Which two diaries are exactly the same?

A

B

C

D

E

F

Answers are on page 76.

Going for gold

In 2004 the Olympic Games are going home! The first ever Olympics were held in Greece over two thousand years ago.

In the beginning

For thousands of years, people have played games and sports. In the time of the Ancient Greeks they began to organise regular festivals of games. One such festival was held every four years in honour of the god Zeus, at Olympia. This was how the Olympic Games began.

Getty Images/Mike Hewitt

Sports days

Today's Olympic Games last for 16 days, and athletes compete in 28 different sports. The first ever Olympic games only lasted one day, but as more events were added they grew longer. This is a typical programme from the ancient Olympics:

Olympic spirit

In ancient days Greece was not one country, but a collection of cities and states that were often at war. All wars stopped while the Olympics lasted and athletes from all states competed in a spirit of peace and friendship.

Day 1
◆Parade of athletes
◆Athletes take the Olympic oath to compete honestly
◆Olympic wreaths made

Day 2
◆Young athletes' events: racing, wrestling and boxing

Day 3
◆Horse races and chariot races
◆Pentathlon

Day 4
◆Sacrifices to Zeus
◆Races
◆Wrestling and boxing
◆Races in armour

Day 5
◆Parade of the winners to the Temple of Zeus
◆Sacrifices to the gods
◆Official banquet

Getty Imags/David Taylor

Getty Images/Hulton Getty

Women compete

Only Greeks could compete in the ancient Olympics – and women were not allowed to enter. Women athletes had their own games called the Heraia, also held every four years. Women first took part in the modern Olympic Games in the year 1900. They were allowed to play 'ladylike' sports such as tennis and golf!

Getty Images/Michael Steele

Long run

The last event in the modern Olympics is the marathon, a 26-mile long race. About two and a half thousand years ago, warriors from Athens were fighting at the Battle of Marathon. When they won, a soldier ran all the way back to Athens – 26 miles away – to take the news of their victory. This year the Olympic marathon will follow the same route that he ran.

Turn to the end of your Annual to have a go at a great marathon game.

Getty Images/Matt Turner

Paralympics

After the main Olympic Games the Paralympics are held. Athletes who have a disability will take part in 18 sporting events. Over 4,000 athletes, representing 125 countries, will compete in 2004.

Food for all seasons

Keep cooking all year round with these great recipes that use seasonal fruits and vegetables.

Summer sizzlers

These tasty veggie kebabs will go perfectly with your burgers at those summer barbecues.

1 Wash the mushrooms, tomatoes and pepper. Carefully cut the pepper and sweetcorn into chun[k]

Ingredients

8 cherry tomatoes ★
8 small mushrooms ★
1 pepper ★ 4 baby
sweetcorn ★ olive oil ★

You need

knife ★ 4 skewers ★
brush ★ disposable
barbecue or grill

Illustrated by Stuart Lynch

2 Thread the vegetables onto the skewers.

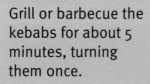

3 Brush the kebabs with a little olive oil.

Grill or barbecue the kebabs for about 5 minutes, turning them once.

4

You can try putting all sorts of other things on your kebabs. How about radishes, chunks of carrot or celery, or even pineapple cubes?

Be safe

Autumn apple feast

Apples are at their most delicious in autumn. Smothering them in chocolate makes them even better!

Winter warmer

Nothing beats a hot baked potato on those cold winter evenings!

Ingredients

1 large potato ★ small tin of baked beans ★ 2 tablespoons grated cheese

You need

fork ★ baking tray ★ knife ★ tablespoon ★ small saucepan

1 Wash and dry your potato. Carefully prick it all over with a fork.

2 Put it on a baking tray. Bake in the oven at 190°C/gas mark 5 for about 1 ¼ hours.

3 When the potato is almost done, gently heat the baked beans in a small saucepan. Mix in the cheese.

4 When your potato is ready, carefully make a cross-shaped cut in the top. Spoon in your filling and eat!

Ingredients

50g chocolate ★ 1 apple ★ hundreds and thousands

You need

heatproof bowl ★ saucepan ★ chopstick ★ knife ★ foil

1 Heat the chocolate in the bowl over simmering water until it is just melted.

Be safe

2 Wash the apple and stick the chopstick firmly into it.

3 Spread the melted chocolate all over the apple. Sprinkle it with hundreds and thousands. Leave it on a piece of kitchen foil until the chocolate has set.

Jane

Lucy

Laura

Katie

Emma

S B

Super Brownie

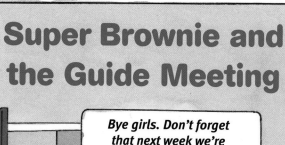

Super Brownie and the Guide Meeting

Bye girls. Don't forget that next week we're staying for the Guides' meeting after ours.

We won't. Bye!

The following week...

Just chat among yourselves, girls. We've got a few minutes before the Guides arrive.

Hi. Nice to have you here.

Thanks for having us.

Hello, girls. Hope you enjoy this evening with us.

Here they come!

This is the Lion Patrol. And this is their Patrol Leader. That's like a Sixer.

Tonight, all our Patrols are working on Go For Its!

What are Go For Its?

They're special themed activity packs that Guides can do. They all get a cool card when they've completed one. Follow me.

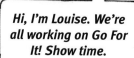

Hi, I'm Louise. We're all working on Go For It! Show time.

Illustrated by Liz McIntosh

Testing time

Science power

Our lives would be very different today without the discoveries made by scientists. How many things in your home are powered by electricity? If scientists had not worked out how to make and use electricity, we would have no fridges, televisions, electric light or many other useful devices.

Science isn't just something you do at school. It is important to all of us in lots of different ways.

Scientific method

Science is all about trying out new ideas. A scientist will have an idea and then do some experiments to test whether the idea really works. It is important to do lots of different experiments, to prove that the idea is right. The scientist must observe experiments closely and record the results with care.

Changing the world

Great scientists change the way we think about the world. Often people don't want to listen to their new ideas. The astronomer Galileo was taken to court for saying that the Earth moves around the sun. Charles Darwin was afraid to publish his new theory of evolution (which claims that people are related to apes) for many years.

Great inventions

Sometimes scientists make discoveries by accident. When Alexander Graham Bell invented the telephone, he was actually trying to find a way of helping deaf people to communicate. He discovered that he could make sound travel a long way by making sound waves into electricity and sending them down a long wire. This was the first telephone.

Try it out

An important part of science is doing experiments. Practise your science skills with this fun experiment.

Float or sink?

Try this experiment to see whether objects float or sink.
Collect all the objects in this list.

apple ⊘ paper clip ⊘ twig ⊘ pencil ⊘ ruler ⊘ penny ⊘ cork ⊘ rubber ⊘ pebble ⊘ marble

Which is the biggest?

Which is the smallest?

Which is the heaviest?

Which is the lightest?

Now try to guess which of the objects will float in water.
Write 'yes' or 'no' in the table, under 'Will it float?'.

	Will it float?	Did it float?
Apple		
Paper clip		
Twig		
Pencil		
Ruler		
Penny		
Cork		
Rubber		
Pebble		
Marble		

It's time to test your guesses! Put the objects into a bowl of water, one at a time. Do they float? Write 'yes' or 'no' in the table, under 'Did it float?'.

In this experiment you have used the skills that a good scientist needs. You had **ideas** about which things would float. You did an **experiment** to test your ideas. You **observed** what happened to the objects in the water. You **recorded** your results and then you **analysed** (thought about) what you have learned.

Take a look at your results.
Were all your guesses right?

Can you tell whether an object will float just by looking at it and weighing it?

Turn to page 76 to find out why some objects sink and others float.

Turn the page to find out what two scientists have to say about their exciting jobs.

Super science

Have you ever thought that science is boring? These women don't – they are both scientists and love their jobs. Read on to find out about their cool careers.

Sweet talk

Emma works for Cadbury Trebor Bassett, where she works out how chocolate and sweets will be made. When the company wants to produce a new type of sweet, it's Emma's job to decide how the factory will make many thousands of them. Of course, she also has to taste the chocolates! Emma finds it very satisfying to see a new kind of chocolate bar come off the production line and then appear in her local shops.

Emma McLeod
Senior Process Development Engineer

Building up

Emma's interest in engineering started at an early age. She always enjoyed making models and helping her dad build things. At school she liked science and maths, and at university she studied Engineering.

Emma says:

'The most important thing about a career is that you enjoy it. If you are good at science and technology and enjoy it, there is no reason why you can't follow a career in it.'

Chocolate Brownie!

For most of her life Emma has been involved in guiding. She was a Brownie, a Guide and a Ranger, then went on to be a Brownie Guider. Her favourite part of Brownies was going on Pack Holiday!

News Team International/Richard Lea-Hair

Julia Rhodes
Wind Farm Manager

Wind power

Julia is an engineer who works on wind farms in this country and in Portugal. Wind farms are groups of tall windmills (called turbines) which make electricity from the power of the wind. They are very good for the environment. Julia visits the farms and makes sure all the turbines are working properly. She loves her job because there is lots of variety and she knows she is working for a cleaner environment.

Science Photo Library/Jeremy Walker

Life's a breeze

Julia's dad is an engineer and she was always interested in his work. When she was about 12 she got hooked on wind power at the Centre for Alternative Technology in Wales. At secondary school she joined the science club, where she got to try all sorts of fun experiments.

Julia says:

'Be yourself and believe in yourself. Determination always pays off but it is important that you enjoy what you have chosen to do.' When she was younger, Julia was a Brownie and was very proud of all the Interest Badges she gained!

Science Photo Library/Chris Knapton

These are just some of the many exciting careers you could have if you study science. For lots more ideas, take a look at the web site www.planet-science.com.

Web safe

Photo tree

You need

green crêpe paper ★ scissors ★
small jam jar ★ sticky tape ★
lump of plasticine ★ fallen stick
with lots of twigs ★ cardboard ★
felt pens or poster paints and
brushes ★ hole punch ★ photos
of friends and family ★ PVA glue
★ thin ribbon or wool

You'll need to go out and find a
fallen stick first. Choose one with
lots of little twigs branching off it.
Remember, look on the ground,
don't break a stick off a living tree.

1

Cut a strip of crêpe
paper long enough to
wrap round the jam jar,
and as wide as the jar is
tall. Cut long snips out
of one edge of the strip,
to make grass. Wrap the
strip around the jar and
stick it in place with
sticky tape.

2

Squish the lump of plasticine
into the jar. Stick the branch
into the plasticine. You might need
to add more plasticine round the
sides to stick it in firmly.

Illustrated by Andi Good

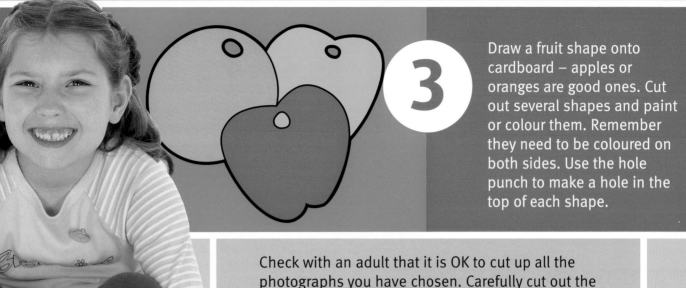

3 Draw a fruit shape onto cardboard – apples or oranges are good ones. Cut out several shapes and paint or colour them. Remember they need to be coloured on both sides. Use the hole punch to make a hole in the top of each shape.

4 Check with an adult that it is OK to cut up all the photographs you have chosen. Carefully cut out the faces of people from your photos. Cut them into lots of different shapes – squares, circles and diamonds. Make sure they are all smaller than your fruit shapes.

5 Stick a cut-out photograph onto each fruit shape. You can stick photos onto both sides of the fruits if you like. Thread a piece of ribbon or wool through the hole and tie the fruits onto your tree.

6 Draw a small leaf shape onto folded crêpe paper and cut it out. Make plenty of leaves in the same way. Stick them onto the twigs with PVA glue.

Turn to page 74 for some handy tips for taking great photos.

Puzzle planet

Go out of this world with these great space mind-bogglers!

Spaced out

These astronauts are enjoying a space walk. But which spaceship is each one attached to?

A

Neil

Buzz

B

C

Helen

Stars in your eyes

How many stars are there in the galaxy?

Across the universe

Which planets are these space travellers going to?

Hannah

'I'm going to the biggest planet.'

'I'll see rings when I get there.'

Michelle

'I'm ready for the red planet.'

'I've got the longest journey.'

Dawn

Banu

Illustrated by Nick Diggory

Star-crossed

Can you fit the names of these star signs into the grid?

Aries
Libra
Virgo
Scorpio
Pisces
Gemini
Leo

Who am I?

Join the dots to find out who lives on this planet!

Missing meteor

Which piece fits the space in the jigsaw?

A
B
C
D
E

Comet's tale

How many planets can you find in the comet's tail?

Happy birthday

**2004 is a special year for Brownies...
you are 90 years old! How much do
you know about Brownies from the
past 90 years?**

In the beginning

Brownies first began in the
year 1914. By then Guides
had been around for four
years. Younger girls, seeing
all the fun the Guides had,
were asking whether they
could join in. So a new
section was set up for them.

Pack facts

The first Brownies didn't have Sixes
– they had patrols. The patrols were
named after British trees. Each patrol
would have had a Guide as a patrol
leader. In those days there might
have been 30 or 40 Brownies in a
Pack. The Brownie badge was in the
shape of an acorn.

Name that Brownie

To start with, girls in the junior section weren't called Brownies
– they were Rosebuds! They didn't like this name much so it
was soon changed. Names like Skylarks, Buds and Bees were
suggested – but the girls liked Brownies best.

Changing clothes

At first, Brownies wore dark blue
uniforms, like the Guides.
However they soon decided that
brown was better for Brownies!
They wore brown dresses with
pockets on, brown ties and
knitted caps. This uniform did not
change very much for 70 years.
In 1990 the brown and yellow
uniforms were introduced, and
Brownies today have an even
bigger choice of clothes to wear.

Photographs by Laura Cartwright

Brownies!

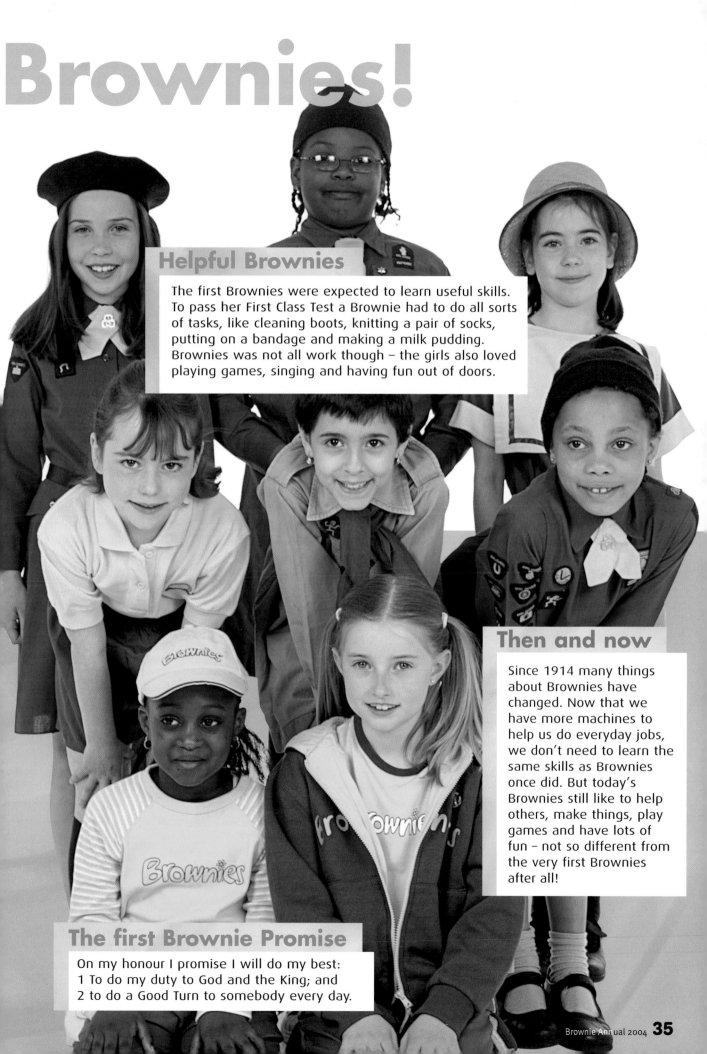

Helpful Brownies

The first Brownies were expected to learn useful skills. To pass her First Class Test a Brownie had to do all sorts of tasks, like cleaning boots, knitting a pair of socks, putting on a bandage and making a milk pudding. Brownies was not all work though – the girls also loved playing games, singing and having fun out of doors.

Then and now

Since 1914 many things about Brownies have changed. Now that we have more machines to help us do everyday jobs, we don't need to learn the same skills as Brownies once did. But today's Brownies still like to help others, make things, play games and have lots of fun – not so different from the very first Brownies after all!

The first Brownie Promise

On my honour I promise I will do my best:
1 To do my duty to God and the King; and
2 to do a Good Turn to somebody every day.

Cosmic cooking

Get set for the space age with these tasty treats.

Mini moons

Ingredients

60g butter ★ 85g sugar ★ 1 egg ★ 1 teaspoon milk ★ ½ tsp vanilla essence ★ 100g self-raising flour ★ 75g plain flour

You need

bowl ★ electric mixer ★ teaspoon ★ sieve ★ rolling pin ★ glass or round cutter ★ baking tray ★ wooden spoon

1 Cream the butter and sugar with the electric mixer until light and fluffy.

2 Add the egg, milk and vanilla and mix well.

3 Sift the self-raising flour in to the bowl and stir in with the wooden spoon. Sift the plain flour and add a little at a time. Mix to a soft dough.

Illustrated by Martina Farrow

4 Put the dough on a floured surface and roll it out to ½cm thick.

5 Cut out dough circles with a glass or round cutter. Then cut out pieces to make half moon and crescent moon shapes.

6 Put the biscuits on a greased baking tray and cook at 180°C/gas mark 4 for about 10 minutes.

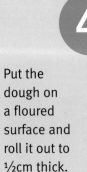

Pizza planets

Ingredients

150g self-raising flour ★ 40g butter or margarine ★ 50g grated cheese ★ 3–4 tablespoons milk ★ small jar tomato sauce or pizza topping ★ 50g 'red' cheese eg Red Leicester ★ 1 red pepper ★ ham, onion, mushrooms, sweetcorn

You need

sieve ★ mixing bowl ★ knife ★ wooden spoon ★ rolling pin ★ chopping board ★ baking tray

1 Sift the flour into the bowl.

2 Chop the butter into small pieces and add it to the bowl. Rub it in with your fingertips until the mixture looks like breadcrumbs.

3 Add the grated cheese and the milk. Mix to a firm dough.

4 Divide the dough into two pieces. Roll them into circles about 10cm across.

5 Spread the tomato sauce over your pizzas and decorate with toppings.

To make Mars, chop the red pepper and ham into small pieces. Scatter them onto the pizza and sprinkle the grated red cheese over the top.

To make Saturn, cover the pizza with grated cheese. Chop the vegetables into small pieces. Arrange them on the pizza in rings.

6 Put the pizzas on a baking tray and cook them for 10–15 minutes at 220°C/gas mark 7.

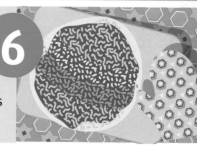

Martian mud

Ingredients

1 ripe banana ★ 1 tablespoon chocolate spread ★ 140ml milk

You need

knife ★ blender ★ glass

Peel and chop the banana. Put it in the blender with the chocolate spread and milk. Whizz until smooth, then pour into a glass and enjoy!

The Bird of the Golden Land

Illustrated by Claire Chrystall

There was once a king, and he lived with his three sons in a castle in a small kingdom by the sea.

Although he was a king he was not very rich, and the only valuable thing he owned was a golden crown. However he was a happy king – he loved his sons and, from time to time, a beautiful bird came and flew around the castle, singing the sweetest song that was ever heard.

One day the king's three sons came to him and said,

'Father, we would all like to get married. Can you find us each a wife?'

The king was worried, because if his sons married he would have to give them each a gift. He did not want them to quarrel over the valuable crown, and he could not choose which son to give it to. So he said,

'I will gladly help you find wives, but first you must help me. Go out and find the beautiful bird that visits me – the Bird of the Golden Land. Whoever brings me the bird will have my golden crown as a wedding gift.'

So the three princes set off together in search of the Bird of the Golden Land. They walked all day and stopped at a cottage to rest for the night.

In the morning, as the princes were getting up, an old man appeared from a corner by the fire. He said to them,

'I know you are searching for the Bird of the Golden Land, and I can help you. Take that hammer, that basket and that rope and follow me.'

> **'Whoever brings me the bird will have my golden crown as a wedding gift'**

So they picked up the hammer, the basket and the rope, and they followed the old man along the road until they came to a large black rock.

'Strike this rock with the hammer,' ordered the old man.

The eldest prince hit the rock with the hammer, and at once it broke apart to reveal a deep, dark hole stretching down into the earth.

'At the bottom of that hole lies the road that leads to the Golden Land,' said the old man. 'Lower yourselves down in the basket – carefully, because it is dangerous.'

The brothers tied the basket onto the rope and the eldest prince jumped in. The others began to lower him down, but it was very dark and scary, and before long he shouted to be pulled up again. The second prince then had a turn, but he too was frightened and asked to be pulled back up.

Finally the youngest prince climbed into the basket and was lowered down the hole. He was nervous, but held on tight and at last he reached the bottom. He set out along the road that leads to the Golden Land.

After walking for a whole day, the prince reached a castle and thought he would ask to stay the night. A young woman came out to meet him.

'I will challenge you to a game'

'I know where you are going,' she said. 'The road to the Golden Land is long, but if you choose the best horse you can find in my stable, you will get there in a single day.'

In the stables the prince found many magnificent, proud horses. However he was not very tall, so he wisely decided that they would all be too big for him. He chose the smallest horse, an ordinary-looking mare, brushed her, saddled her and led her outside.

'Well done,' said the young woman. 'You have chosen the best horse in the stable. She will take you to the Golden Land in a day.'

So the prince said goodbye and rode off. After a long ride, when the mare trotted calmly over both land and sea, she spoke to him, saying,

'Look ahead, young prince, and tell me what you can see.'

'I see a large castle with many towers,' replied the prince.

'That is the castle of the King of the Golden Land. The bird you seek belongs to him.'

The prince rode up to the castle, stabled his mare and paid a visit to the king.

'So,' shouted the king irritably, 'I know why you are here, young man. You have come to steal away my beautiful sweet-singing bird. Well, I will challenge you to a game. At sunrise tomorrow I will hide myself. If you can find me by sunset, you shall have the bird. If you fail, I will chop off your head!'

The prince went sadly back to the stable and spoke to his mare.

'Whatever shall I do? How can I find the king and win the bird for my father?'

'Don't worry,' replied the mare comfortingly. 'Go to sleep here in my stable, and in the morning I will help you.'

So the prince curled up in the warm straw and slept soundly. In the morning the mare woke him and whispered to him,

'Go to the apple orchard. On the tallest tree there is a large red apple. Cut this in half, and you will find the king.'

So the prince did as he was told. As he picked the apple, the king's daughter spoke to him.

'You come to steal my father's bird, and now you are taking his finest apple!'

'If you want some I will only take half of it, and

leave half for you,' the prince replied, and he sliced the apple in half. Out leapt the king, in a fine fury.

'Ouch! You have cut me on the head! You were lucky today, but tomorrow I will hide again. If you cannot find me, I will chop off your head.'

The prince returned to the horse's stable and slept there in the straw. She woke him in the morning and whispered to him,

'Go to the kitchen and ask for a bowl of soup. Then go to the cupboard to look for a spoon. In there you will find a pin. Cut it in half to find the king.'

So the prince found the castle kitchens and asked politely for a bowl of soup. He went to the cupboard and inside it, just as the mare had said, there was a pin. As he took it out the king's daughter said,

'Oh! Surely you are not going to take away that lovely pin.'

'Well, I was going to – but if you insist, I will leave you half of it. Half is better than nothing.'

With this, the prince cut the pin in half, and out hopped the king, jumping up and down in rage.

'Ouch! Ouch! You have cut my head again! I will give you one final chance – and if you cannot find me tomorrow, I really will chop off your head!'

'I'll hide you so secretly that the king will never find you'

The next morning the little mare whispered,

'Take these grains down to the lake and feed them to the duck that lives there. Ask her to lay an egg for you. In that egg you will find the king.'

At the side of the lake, the prince threw down his grain and the duck swam over to eat it. He picked her up and asked her to lay him an egg.

'Indeed, I do not wish to lay an egg,' quacked the duck.

'Well I will not let you go until you do,' said the prince, and he held onto the duck until she got fed up and laid a large egg.

'What a delicious looking egg,' remarked the king's daughter, strolling past. 'I would like it for my breakfast. Surely you will not take a simple egg away from me?'

'I rather fancy an egg myself. Shall we share it?' asked the prince, and he cracked the egg in half. At once the king sprang out, rubbing his forehead and spluttering with anger.

'That is three times that you have cracked open my head! I will not stand for any more of this. Tomorrow it is your turn to hide – and as soon as I find you I will chop off your head!'

The prince returned sadly to his mare's stable.

'What am I to do? You have helped me find the king three times. Now will you help me hide somewhere tomorrow?'

'Don't worry,' said the horse. 'I'll hide you so secretly that the king will never find you.'

When morning came, she woke the prince and quickly turned him into a flea. The king soon arrived at the stable and searched it all day long, but he never noticed the tiny flea hopping in the straw.

The next day, the mare turned the prince into a bee. Again the king searched all day long, but could not find him. On the third day the mare turned the prince into one of her own eyelashes, and though the king searched until the sun set, he could not find the youngest prince. He stormed back up to his castle in a terrible temper.

'Go up to the castle now,' whispered the mare, quickly turning the prince back into himself. 'The king will be tired out with all his searching and anger. When he falls asleep, take the bird in its cage and we can ride away together.'

The prince was rather afraid of losing his head, but he crept bravely up to the castle. Inside all was silent, for when the king slept so did all the court. The prince took up the beautiful bird in her cage, and tiptoed away. As he went, however, the bird sang one single note. At once the whole court woke and cried out, 'Thief!'

The prince fled to his mare and jumped onto her back. They galloped away with the king's army after them. They flew over land and sea, and at last they left the army behind.

As they trotted up to the castle where the horse had come from, the same young woman came to meet them.

'Well done, young prince!' she cried. 'You have rescued the Bird of the Golden Land from her captivity. Now I can tell you that she, and the mare you rode on, and I myself, are all queens. This bird is the most powerful of us and she can change into a bird whenever she wishes.'

As she said this the bird and the mare both changed into queens. All four of them set off together for the bottom of the deep hole.

> ## 'You have rescued the Bird of the Golden Land'

Two of the queens jumped into the basket and called for the princes to pull them up. The most powerful queen stayed at the bottom with the youngest prince. This was a good idea, because as soon as the older brothers saw the two queens, they fell deeply in love and forgot all about the youngest prince. They set straight off for their father's castle with their queens.

The king was delighted to see them, but worried about his youngest son.

'Where is he? You have found wives but lost your brother, and you have not brought me the Bird of the Golden Land.'

Back at the bottom of the deep hole, the most powerful queen had turned herself into a bird and flown to the top, where she became a woman again and pulled up the prince in the basket. They hurried back to the castle, where they found the king and told him everything.

The king was overjoyed to have his son back, and happy that the Bird of the Golden Land now lived in his own castle. The queen didn't mind becoming a bird and singing for the king whenever he wished, and they all lived together very happily, in the castle in the small kingdom by the sea.

Miss Dorothy

Hi, I'm Dorothy Com. My friends call me Dot Com because I have my own web site, at **www.missdorothy.com.** Why not drop in and visit me there?
I don't spend all my time on the Internet though – I also love to get out and about with my friends. But whether I'm in or out, it's important to keep myself safe. Have a go at my quiz and find out how much you know about safety!

Illustrated by Matt McArdle. © missdorothy.com

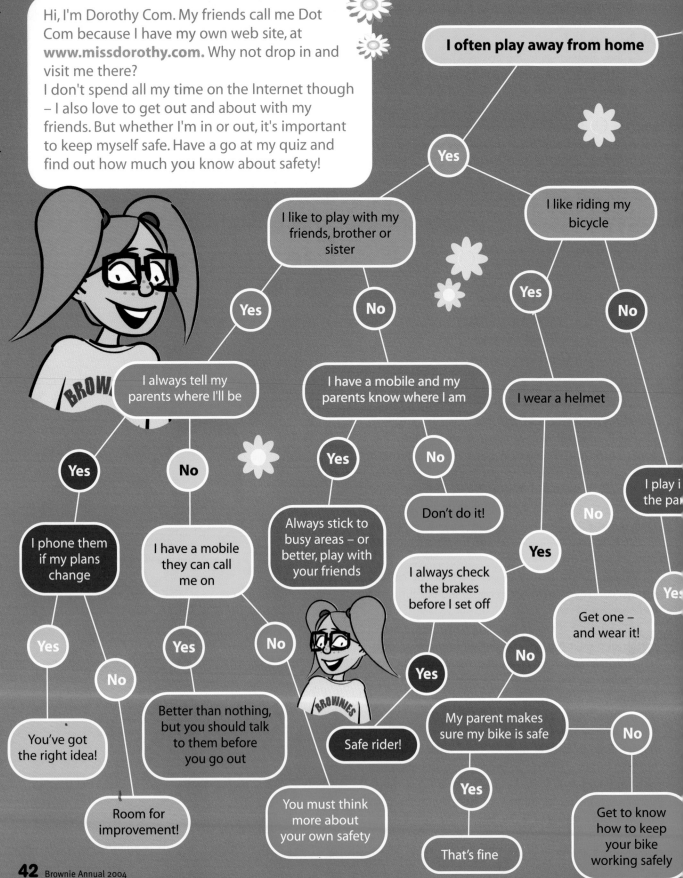

I often play away from home

Yes

I like to play with my friends, brother or sister

I like riding my bicycle

Yes

No

Yes

No

I always tell my parents where I'll be

I have a mobile and my parents know where I am

I wear a helmet

Yes

No

Yes

No

Don't do it!

I play i the pa

No

Yes

Yes

I phone them if my plans change

I have a mobile they can call me on

Always stick to busy areas – or better, play with your friends

I always check the brakes before I set off

Get one – and wear it!

Ye

Yes

No

Yes

No

Yes

No

You've got the right idea!

Better than nothing, but you should talk to them before you go out

Safe rider!

My parent makes sure my bike is safe

No

Room for improvement!

You must think more about your own safety

Yes

Get to know how to keep your bike working safely

That's fine

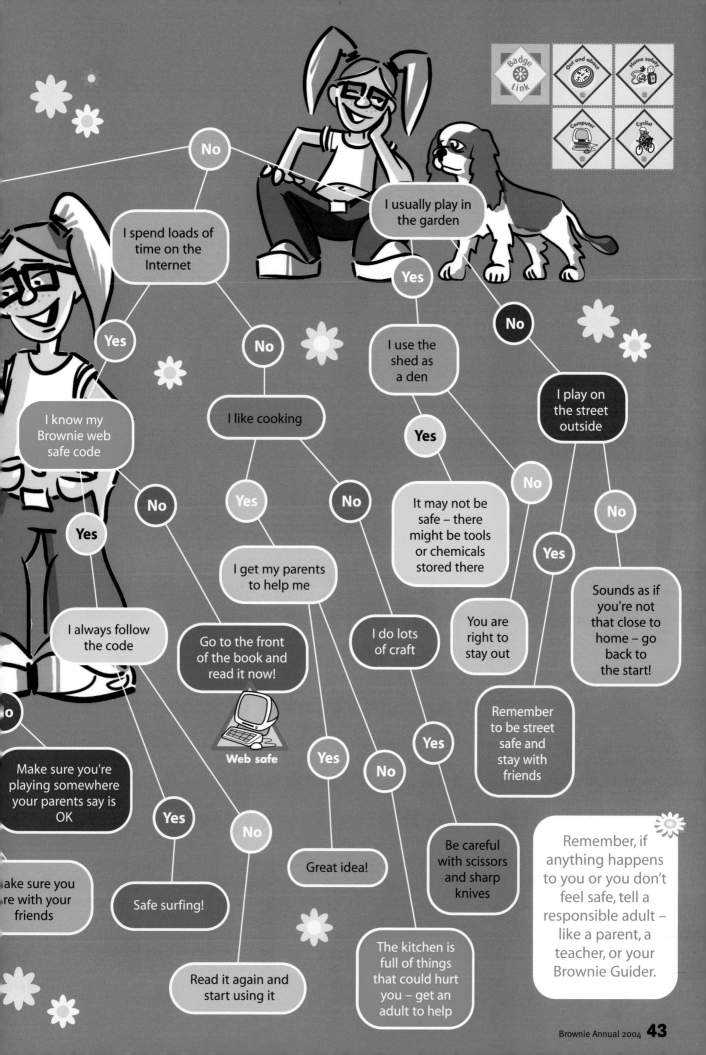

Funky monkeys

2004 is the Chinese Year of the Monkey. Celebrate by finding out all about these loveable animals.

Friendly creatures

Did you know that there are over 160 different kinds of monkey? Most of them live in Africa, Asia and the forests of South America. Monkeys live together in groups, called 'troops'. They make friends by grooming each other's fur.

Little monkeys!

Monkey babies are born with strong fingers so they can cling to their mothers' fur. They hitch a ride with their mothers or fathers for the first few months. Other adult monkeys are very interested in babies. Some monkey mums let the other grown-ups babysit while they have a rest!

NHPA/Mike Lane

Brain boxes

Among the cleverest monkeys are the capuchins of South America. They have learned to crack open nuts and even shellfish by banging them on trees. Some capuchins have even been trained to fetch and carry things for people in wheelchairs.

NHPA/James Carmichael Jr

Lion in danger

The beautiful golden lion tamarin, from Brazil, is one of the most endangered monkeys. There are few left in the wild because their rainforest home is being destroyed by humans.

NHPA/Mark Bowler

Small is beautiful

Marmosets and tamarins are the smallest monkeys – about the size of squirrels. Many of them are brightly coloured. The tiny pygmy marmoset only weighs 100g. It feeds on gum, which it gets by scraping holes in trees so the gum oozes out.

Noisy neighbours

Howler monkeys are large leaf-eaters. They get their name from the very loud roaring noises they make to protect their territories. Male howler monkeys have a space in their throats which vibrates, making a noise that can be heard from miles away.

NHPA/Kevin Schafer

NHPA/Jonathan and Angela Scott

Lucky langurs

Hanuman langurs live in India, where they are sacred to Hindus. They are named after the Hindu monkey-god Hanuman. Many live in or near to temples, and on sacred days people come to feed them.

Bath time!

The Japanese macaque lives further north than all other monkeys. Its thick furry coat keeps it warm in snowy weather. Just like us, it also enjoys a hot bath! These unusual monkeys soak in hot springs on chilly days.

NHPA/Andy Rouse

Plain living

Baboons make their home in the grassy plains of Africa. They have lived on the ground for so long that they now find it hard to climb trees. Baboons will eat almost anything but their favourite food is fruit.

Looking up

Have you ever been stuck in a crowd with tall people in front of you, so you couldn't see what was going on? Make this handy periscope and you'll never have that problem again! It will help you see things that are usually too high.

You need

A4 piece of card ★ ruler ★ pencil ★ scissors ★ masking tape ★ 2 small mirrors ★ poster paints

Illustrated by Andi Good

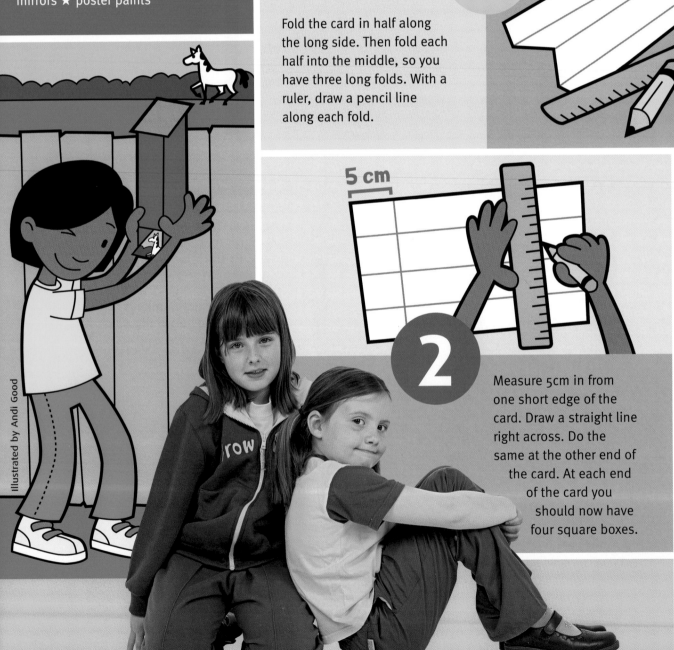

1

Fold the card in half along the long side. Then fold each half into the middle, so you have three long folds. With a ruler, draw a pencil line along each fold.

5 cm

2

Measure 5cm in from one short edge of the card. Draw a straight line right across. Do the same at the other end of the card. At each end of the card you should now have four square boxes.

Use your ruler to draw diagonal lines across four of the squares, just like on the diagram. Take your time and make sure the lines are in the right places.

3

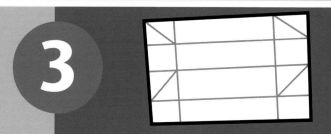

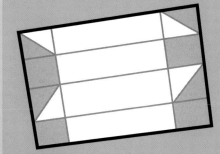

Now carefully cut along the lines so you cut off the pieces that are coloured grey in the diagram.

4

Fold up your periscope to make a tube. Carefully stick the edges together with masking tape. (If you use ordinary sticky tape you will not be able to paint over it when you decorate your finished periscope.)

5

Stick your two small mirrors to the sloping ends of your periscope, so the mirrors are on the inside. If the mirrors are too small, stick them on to pieces of cardboard first. It does not matter if they are a bit too big.

6

Now decorate your periscope! Paint it in bright colours and patterns.

7

Watch the birdie

If you have a bird feeder in your garden, use your periscope to help you watch the birds. Paint it in splodgy patterns with green and brown paint. This will make it difficult to see against trees and bushes. Then hide behind a bush and stick your periscope up. You can watch the birds and squirrels without scaring them away.

How it works

Light comes in at the top of the periscope and gets reflected off the top mirror, then the bottom mirror. It comes out at the bottom, where your eyes are!

Competition

Going to the seaside is always fun! Every year, people take more than 25 million holidays and 110 million day trips at the British seaside. The UK has a lot of coastline – there are 10,500 miles of seaside to choose from!

Trips to the seaside are all about having fun, but every year lots of accidents happen. To help keep you safe at the seaside, a national campaign called Sea Smart has been set up. Sea Smart aims to help reduce the number of accidents that happen at the coast.

Sea Smart is organised by the Maritime and Coastguard Agency (MCA), the organisation that deals with emergencies at the coast. Each year, coastguards help thousands of people on the UK coastline. Coastguards save an average of twelve lives a day.

Being careful at the seaside can stop many accidents. Always remember these important points from the Sea Smart Code:

☆ If you see anyone in trouble, dial 999 and ask for the coastguard.
☆ Check the weather and tides before you leave.
☆ Keep close to an adult all the time.
☆ Always tie inflatables to an adult on the shore.
☆ Keep clear of cliff edges – they can be slippery when wet.
☆ Don't drink and drown – eating and drinking before swimming may give you cramps.

So have fun at this seaside this year – just make sure you're safe and Sea Smart.

Web safe

For more information about Sea Smart, visit www.mcga.gov.uk.

Win a trip to a Sea Life Centre!

Talk to your Guider before sending your entry.

Girlguiding UK has teamed up with Sea Smart and Sea Life for this fantastic competition. You could win free entry to your nearest Sea Life Centre for your whole Pack. To enter, either send us a drawing of the most fantastic sandcastle you can imagine or create the real thing and send us a photo.

On the back of your entry, write:
☆ **your name**
☆ **your age**
☆ **your address**
☆ **your Brownie Pack**
☆ **the best three things in your Brownie Annual**
☆ **the best thing about being a Brownie**

Hurry! The closing date is 16 February 2004!

Send your entry to:

Brownie Annual 2004
Sea Smart Competition
Girlguiding UK
17–19 Buckingham Palace Road
London SW1W 0PT

Each Sea Life Centre offers plenty of variety for everyone to enjoy. Talks, feeding displays and demonstrations take you to the very depths of the seas on an amazing voyage of discovery. More information about each of the Sea Life Centres can be found on www.sealife.co.uk.

Web safe

The winning entry will be selected by the Coastguard. The judges' decision is final and no correspondence will be entered into. The prize consists of: free entry for the winner and her Brownie Pack to a UK Sea Life Centre of their choice; a trip to a local Coastguard station; and a Sea Smart goody bag for each member of the Pack. The prize will be valid for 12 months. Transport and accommodation are not included in the prizes.

Mind-bogglers

Don't get hot and bothered – chill out with these cool puzzles.

Warm words

Rearrange these letters to make a word. Then see how many words of three letters or more you can make from it.

M U R T T E E R P R A E E A

Get the hump

Can you help this thirsty camel find her way to the oasis?

Penguin puzzler

Three of these penguins are different from the rest. Can you spot them?

Fun in the sun

These girls are trying to cool off on a hot day. Can you spot 10 differences between the pictures?

Cool countries?

Find a hot country and a cold country in each line. The letters are in the correct order.

```
C M A E N X I A D C O A
G R E E I N D N I L A N D A
B S R A W E Z D E I L N
I C E G Y E L P A N T D
N K O R E W N A Y Y A
```

Hot spots

Which two leopards are exactly the same?

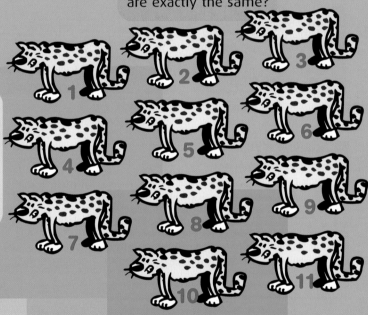

Muffler muddle

In what order would you have to pick up the scarves so that you take the top one each time?

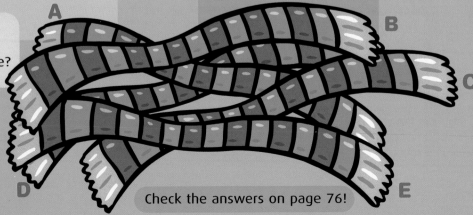

Check the answers on page 76!

Portugal

Get the facts on this small but fascinating country.

Sunshine state

Portugal has fine weather almost all year round. The wettest season is from November to March. Some parts of the country can get very hot in summer. Many people go on holiday to the sunny beaches in the south of Portugal. Water sports, like swimming and surfing, are very popular.

Sarah Melrose

Party time

One of Portugal's biggest events is Carnaval, which takes place about six weeks before Easter. It involves partying, parading and painted faces. In June it's time for the Festa de São João, when people dance through the streets and hit each other over the head with leeks!

Euro 2004

The football competition Euro 2004 is being held in eight cities in Portugal. This will be the first major championship that Portugal has hosted. The Portuguese love football and are proud of their many talented footballers, like Luis Figo and Rui Costa. Five football stadiums are being rebuilt especially for Euro 2004.

Getty Images/Claire Brunskill

Spice of life

During the Middle Ages, Portugal was one of the richest countries in Europe. The Portuguese were great sailors and explorers. They were the first Europeans to sail around Africa to the Indian Ocean. There they bought spices like cinnamon, cloves, nutmeg and pepper. These spices were very rare in Europe, so they were expensive. Portugal became very wealthy from the spice trade.

Sail away

Famous Portuguese explorers include Ferdinand Magellan, who led the first expedition to sail all the way round the world. Vasco da Gama was the first European to sail to India. Prince Henry 'the Navigator' was interested in exploration and built a school for sailors to learn the skills of navigation.

Science Photo Library/George Bernard

Brownies recycle

Cork production is a very environmentally friendly industry. In 2000, Guides and Brownies in the UK helped to collect and recycle more than a million corks! This project helped to protect the cork forests in Portugal by proving that cork can easily be recycled.

NHPA/Vincente Garcia Conseco

Top trees

Portugal is the world's biggest producer of cork. For over a thousand years people have been harvesting cork from cork oak trees. Skilled cutters carefully strip off the bark then paint the date on to the tree. The tree must be left for ten years before it can be harvested again. The cork bark is made into products like cork tiles and bottle stoppers.

Little Birds

Portuguese Brownies are called Avezinhas, which means Little Birds. Avezinhas are aged from six to ten. Their badge is a feather and their motto is 'A Little Bird always helps'.

NHPA/Mike Lane

Lovely lynx

Portugal has some beautiful animals, like the rare Iberian lynx. Lynxes are medium-sized members of the cat family with pointed ears, short tails and spotted fur. The Iberian lynx lives in woodland, especially cork oak forests, and hunts rabbits for food.

Greek treats

Meze is a meal made from lots of appetisers. It is popular in Greece and other Mediterranean and Middle Eastern countries. Have a go at making some of these delicious dishes!

Ingredients

1 can of chickpeas, drained ★ 1 garlic clove, crushed ★ 1 tablespoon tahini (sesame seed paste, available at most supermarkets and health food stores) ★ 2 tablespoons olive oil ★ 3 tablespoons milk

You need

A food processor or blender

Yummy hummus

Hummus is a savoury spread that tastes really good served with warm pitta bread, tortilla chips, crisps, or even jacket potatoes.

Put all the ingredients into a blender or food processor and blitz until creamy.

Tasty tzatziki

Ingredients

half a cucumber ★ juice of ½ lemon ★ olive oil ★ 1 garlic clove ★ 1 small pot natural yoghurt

You need

cheese grater ★ bowl ★ tablespoon ★ garlic press ★ cling film

1 Wash and carefully grate the cucumber. Put it in the bowl, and add the lemon juice and 1 tablespoon of olive oil.

Crush the garlic and add it to the bowl. Now add the yoghurt and mix everything together really well.

2

3

Cover the bowl with cling film and chill in the fridge for an hour. Serve chilled with warm pitta.

Illustrated by Stuart Lynch

Ingredients

1 cup warm water ★ 2 teaspoons active dried yeast ★ ½ teaspoon sugar ★ 1 teaspoon salt ★ 345g self-raising flour ★ olive oil

You need

large bowl ★ wooden spoon ★ tablespoon ★ baking sheet ★ floured board

Pitta bread

Pitta is a soft, flat bread that is especially popular in Greece. You can split it and add all sorts of fillings for a tasty sandwich.

1 Pour the water into a large bowl, and add the yeast. Stir in the sugar and salt, and add the flour a tablespoonful at a time.

2 Mix the ingredients together with a spoon and then bring the dough together into a ball in the bowl with your hands.

3 Place the dough on a floured surface, and knead for 10 minutes or until the dough feels springy.

4 Smear a little oil around the bowl, and roll the ball of dough around until it is covered. Leave it in a warm place, and let it rise until it is about twice the size it was.

5 Heat the oven to about 230°C/gas mark 8. Punch the dough to knock out some of the air and divide it into six pieces. Roll the balls into rounds about 5mm thick and place them on a baking sheet so they are not touching.

6 Bake the breads for about 10 minutes. Take them out of the oven very carefully, as they will be hot, and may have hot steam inside.

I've seen the tallest lady –
She's like a walking crane!
Her neck is like a steeple
And her head's the weather vane!

Or else it's like a ladder
Propped up against a wall,
And from the top she peers down
And we look very small!

Some people think she's snooty
With her nose stuck in the sky;
But I expect she's lonely
Up aloft, and shy.

The sparrows say she's beautiful –
Only the sparrows know!
What a waste of beauty
Not to let it show!

I'm going to coax her gently
– She knows I understand –
One day, she'll bend her head
   right down
And eat out of my hand.

Gina Wilson

'Madame Giraffe' from JIM-JAM PYJAMAS by Gina Wilson published by Jonathan
Cape. Used by permission of The Random House Group Limited.

Perfect pets

Gerbils can be fun and friendly pets. Read on to find out how to give these little animals a happy life.

RSPCA/Mike Lane

In the wild

Gerbils come from the deserts of Mongolia, in Asia. They live in tunnels underground where they can hide from the hot summer sun and keep warm in cold weather. In summer they gather seeds, grass and plants and store them in their tunnels to eat in winter.

Best of friends

Gerbils like company and they should never have to live on their own. It's best to get two brothers or sisters from the same litter. They will be used to each other and won't fight.

Clean teeth

Like all rodents, gerbils have long teeth that grow all the time, so they need a piece of wood to gnaw. This keeps their teeth healthy.

RSPCA/Angela Hampton

Fast asleep

Your gerbils will need some paper bedding so they can make a comfy nest to sleep in. They sleep at nights but also like to have a rest in the daytime. In the wild they would sleep at midday to keep out of the hot sun.

Happy home

Gerbils can be kept in a large cage but a gerbilarium is much better. This is a glass tank, like a big fish tank, with a deep layer of burrowing material in the bottom. Your gerbils can build tunnels and a nest just like they would in the wild. You can look through the glass and watch them digging away!

Holding and stroking

Gerbils are friendly animals and most of them enjoy being gently stroked and handled. Pick up gerbils by cupping them in the palms of your hands. Hold them over a table or your lap so if they suddenly jump they won't get hurt. Never grab a gerbil by its tail.

RSPCA/Angela Hampton

RSPCA/Angela Hampton

RSPCA/Angela Hampton

RSPCA/Mike Lane

Playtime

Gerbils are very lively little animals. They love to explore and play with new toys. Pet shops sell lots of toys for gerbils but a toilet roll tube can be just as much fun. Toys to climb on and wriggle through will give your gerbils plenty to do.

Feeding time

In the wild, gerbils eat seeds, grains and plants. You can buy gerbil mixes of seeds and nuts from a pet shop. Your pets will also love fresh treats like banana, apple, cabbage or cheese. Feeding gerbils treats from your hand will help them learn to love you!

Riding high

Riding is a popular and exciting Olympic sport.

Getty images/Matt Turner

Exciting eventing

Equestrian events (events which involve horses) are part of the Olympic tradition. In the ancient Olympics, horse races and chariot races were very popular. Today, the horses and riders take part in three-day eventing. This involves three different competitions: dressage, show jumping and endurance.

Getty images/Al Bello

Dressage

For the dressage event, horses and riders learn a sequence of movements like walking, trotting and turning. Dressage shows how well the horse and rider work together. The horse needs to be obedient and the rider must have very good control.

Jumping

Show jumping competitions have been taking place for two hundred years. Jumping tests the energy and skill of the horse. Horses and riders go round a course of 15 to 20 jumps. They lose points if a horse knocks off part of a jump, or lands in a water jump.

Endurance

The endurance event is a long ride across country. There are also jumps on parts of the course. The event is timed, and teams lose points if they take too long to finish it. Horses and riders must be very strong and fit to take part.

Animal athletes

Horses taking part in the Olympics must be at least seven years old. Each horse must come from the same country as its rider. When the medals are awarded, both the horse and the rider are declared winners.

Horse power

Three-day eventing became an Olympic sport in 1912. Since then Great Britain has won five gold, eight silver and nine bronze medals in the event. At the 2000 Olympics in Australia, Britain's equestrian team won the silver medal. Riding is the only Olympic sport in which men and women compete together.

Find out more

It takes many long years of training to become an Olympic champion. However there are lots of competitions for young riders. The Pony Club holds many events for members – check out their web site on www.pcuk.org. If you're at all interested in learning to ride, you can find British Horse Society approved riding stables at www.bhs.org.uk.

Web safe

Feathered friends

Brighten up a dull corner with this airy mobile.

You need

10 paper pulp balls, 5 large and 5 small ★ needles and cotton ★ PVA glue ★ poster paints and brushes ★ 15 coloured feathers ★ scraps of felt ★ scissors ★ 1m of very thin elastic

Illustrated by Beccy Blake

1

Using a thick needle, carefully make a hole all the way through a large paper pulp ball. Tie a knot in one end of a length of cotton and thread it up through the hole.

2

Glue a smaller ball on to the side of the large one, to make the bird's head. Hang it up with the thread to let the glue dry. Make four more birds in the same way.

3

Carefully paint your birds and hang them up to dry.

4

When the paint is dry, make a hole at the back of one bird's body and push in a feather for the tail. Make another hole on each side of the body and push in feathers for the wings. Make sure you get the holes level.

Draw or paint an eye on each side of the bird's head. Cut a beak from a small piece of felt and stick it to the front of the head. Decorate the other birds in the same way.

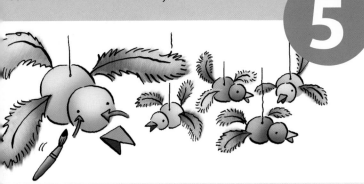

5

Thread the long piece of elastic on to a needle and tie a knot in the end. Take all the cotton threads out of the birds. Thread one bird on to the elastic and push it down to the bottom. Tie a knot in the elastic, about 10cm above the bird. Thread on the next bird and push it down to the knot.

6

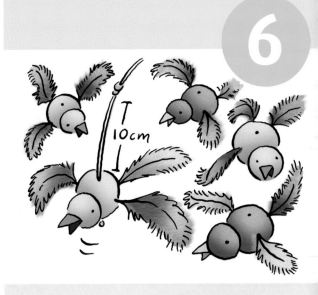

10cm

7

Keep tying knots and threading on the birds until they are all on the elastic. If you gently tug the bottom bird they will all flutter. Now find somewhere to hang up your pretty mobile!

Best buddies

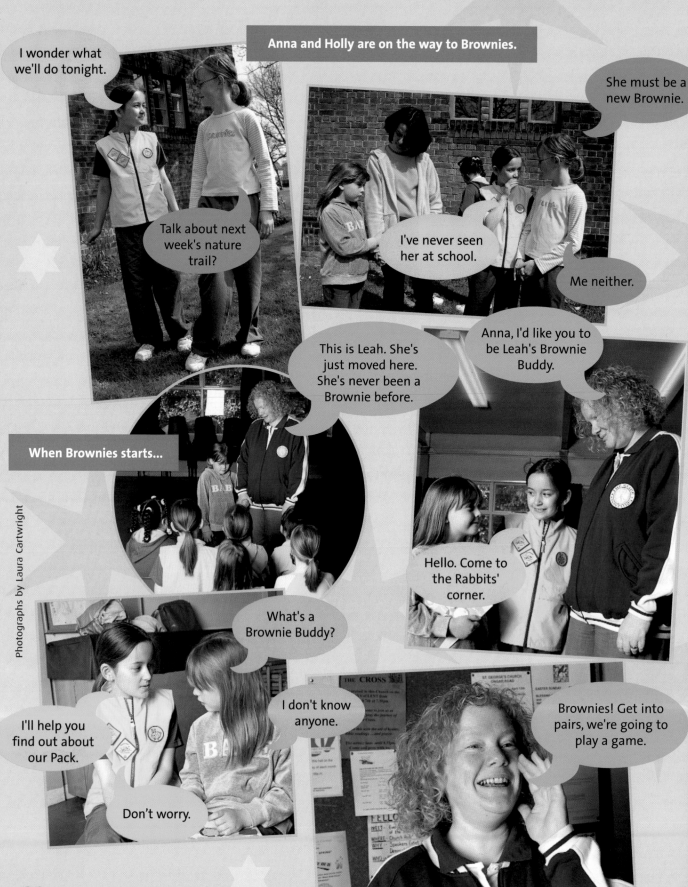

Photographs by Laura Cartwright

Photographs by Laura Cartwright

Brownie twisters

Can you get your mind around these puzzles based on Brownie traditions?

Knotty problem

These Brownies have got in a tangle practising their knots! Can you find out which ball of string belongs to which Brownie?

Jenny   Jo   Ann

A   B   C

Word search

Can you find all these words to do with Brownie traditions?

Flag
Compass
Rosebud
Uniform
Knot
Matches
Scarf
Pockets
Owl
Toadstool

A	R	Q	P	N	K	C	I	H	C	H	A
M	F	U	N	I	F	O	R	M	T	E	T
J	Z	L	C	X	W	M	X	V	W	T	B
Q	U	L	A	L	S	P	V	N	O	S	R
R	W	Z	C	G	M	A	L	A	R	C	X
P	O	C	K	E	T	S	D	O	F	U	A
I	K	M	O	R	O	S	E	B	U	D	L
A	C	F	Y	W	T	V	C	S	J	T	B
F	K	S	R	O	V	X	B	A	L	P	R
H	P	N	O	Z	R	M	K	N	R	X	O
I	T	L	O	Z	V	A	Q	J	G	F	N
A	J	M	A	T	C	H	E	S	L	T	F

Flag break

Which puzzle piece will finish the Union flag jigsaw?

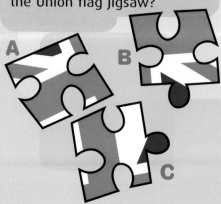

A   B   C

D   E   F

Mixed signals

Which two Brownies are signalling the same letter?

Scrambled Sixes

Can you unscramble these letters to find the names of some Six emblems?

DHAWBBCO
MOGEN
TISPER
MIP
IXIPE
PECHRALUNE
LIPEEK
DUGHLIHIEL

To the point

Which compass has all the points in the correct place?

Double trouble

Cross out all the letters that appear more than once. Rearrange the ones that are left to find out an old name for Brownies.

M S K L F E
L T A M D N
U F T C W A
W M B F L T
O N R K W C

The answers are on page 76.

Time out

**Find out all about time and dates.
After all, time flies when you're having fun!**

Day by day

How many days in a year? If you think there are 365, you are almost right! In fact, there are 365 and a quarter. Because we can't have quarter days, they are saved up, and every fourth year they are used to make an extra day: February 29th. Years with an extra day, like 2004, are called leap years.

In a spin

Earth races through space at about 100,000 kilometres an hour. While it is moving it also spins around. One spin lasts for one day, or 24 hours. Actually, the Earth now spins more slowly than it used to, so days are getting longer. A dinosaur's day would have been half an hour shorter than our day.

Long years

Our year is the length of time it takes for the Earth to travel once around the Sun. Other planets have longer or shorter years than Earth. On Mercury, the planet nearest to the Sun, a year is just 88 Earth days long. Jupiter's year is almost 12 Earth years long. One year on Pluto, the planet furthest from the Sun, lasts for 248 Earth years!

Round the world

In ancient times, people believed that the Sun and all the stars moved around the Earth. This did not change until 1543 when a Polish man named Nicholas Copernicus suggested that Earth orbited the Sun. Many people thought this was a crazy idea and it was a long time before scientists proved that Copernicus was right.

Science Photo Library/John Sanford

Star time

The first people to start measuring the time with calendars were the ancient Egyptians. They based their calendars on the movements of the stars, and used them to work out when to plant crops.

Science Photo Library/Lorenz Denney

Foolish fact!

Have you ever wondered why April 1st is called April Fool's Day? In France, the year once began on April 1st. Then, in 1564, the king decided that the year would start from January. However, not everyone liked this and some people still celebrated the new year on April 1st. They were known as April Fools!

Science Photo Library/Tony Craddock

Different dates

Not everyone in the world uses the same sort of calendar to work out the date. There are as many as 40 different calendars being used today. In the Chinese calendar, years are named after animals. The Muslim calendar is based on the movements of the Moon around the Earth.

Turn to page 16 for some great leap year puzzles.

Olympic feasts

Flaming torch

Ingredients

1 packet of orange jelly ★ 1 small tin of mandarin oranges ★ 1 tub of chocolate ice cream

You need

cling film ★ bowl ★ spoon ★ plate ★ fork

1 Make up an orange jelly according to the packet instructions. Mix a small tin of mandarin oranges into the jelly. Leave it to set.

2 Line the bowl with cling film. Push it right against the bowl to get rid of the creases.

3 Spoon the ice cream into the bowl and push it down firmly. Leave a hollow in the top. Put it in the freezer and chill for two hours.

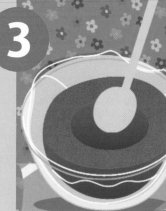

4 Take the ice cream bowl out of the freezer. Turn it upside down over a plate and lift the bowl off. Peel off the cling film and turn the ice cream the other way up.

5 Mash the orange jelly with a fork and pile it into the ice cream hollow. Pile it high so it looks like orange flame leaping up from the Olympic torch. Now tuck in before the ice cream melts!

Javelins

Throwing the javelin was an event in the ancient Olympics, and it is still done today. You won't want to throw these tasty javelins away!

Ingredients

1 packet puff pastry ★
60g grated cheese ★
a little milk ★ paprika

You need

rolling pin ★ pastry brush ★ knife ★ baking tray

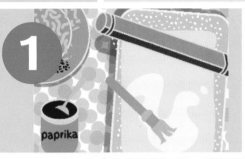

1 Roll out the puff pastry into a rectangle 25cm by 20cm. Brush it with milk. Scatter about two-thirds of the cheese over half of the rectangle. Sprinkle with a pinch of paprika.

2 Fold the plain half of the pastry over the cheese. Roll it flat.

3 Cut the pastry into long thin strips. Cut one end of each strip to a point. Put the strips onto a baking tray, brush them with milk and sprinkle the rest of the cheese over them.

4 Cook the javelins at 200°C/gas mark 6 for 12–15 minutes until they are crisp and golden.

Medal cakes

Ingredients

12 small cakes ★
125g icing sugar ★ about
1 tablespoon water ★
yellow colouring ★
1 tablespoon cocoa powder ★ yellow, brown and white sweets and cake decorations

You need

sieve ★ bowl ★ spoon ★ knife

1 Sift the icing sugar into the bowl. Gradually mix in the water until you have smooth icing. Ice four of the cakes with the white icing.

2 Mix a few drops of yellow food colouring into the icing. Ice four more of the cakes.

3 Mix the cocoa powder into the icing and ice the last four cakes. Now decorate them to make gold, silver and bronze medals. Use yellow sweets and decorations on the gold cakes; white chocolate drops and silver balls on the silver; and chocolate drops on the bronze medals.

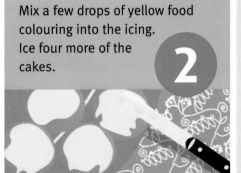

Illustrated by Martina Farrow

photo fun

These top tips will help you take great photos.

Which way up?

A photograph can be taken either sideways (known as landscape format) or upright (portrait). Look at the subject and decide which is better. For a countryside view, use landscape. If you're taking a picture of a single person or the Eiffel Tower, you should use portrait format.

Fill the frame

Try to fill the whole picture with your subject. To take a picture of a horse, for example, move in close so it is big enough to fill up the frame. If you want a picture of a field and trees with a horse or two included, stand well back.

Think before you shoot!

Which way up should the camera go – portrait or landscape?

Will the picture look more interesting if you take a step to the side, or crouch down?

What is in the background – have you got a lamp post growing out of someone's head?

Check the edges of the picture – is there anything that shouldn't be in the picture?

Look carefully through the viewfinder of your camera. The picture you see here is the picture your camera will take.

Try to vary the kinds of photograph you take. Look out for elements like these:

Look for interesting shapes

Photographing an object against a plain background will show off its shape.

Texture

Close-up photographs of texture can work very well. The grain of the wood on an old garden shed can be beautiful and colourful.

Reflection

Look at mirrors, shiny metal or water to find reflections. Take pictures in the rain and catch the glistening streets, or wait until it has just stopped and photograph the images in the puddles.

Frame

Include a natural frame in the picture, such as a cat sitting in a window, or the view through a gap in a hedge.

Detail

Sometimes it's interesting to pick out one part of a subject rather than the whole, for example the handle and lock of a church door.

Patterns

Look out for repeating patterns, such as rows of deckchairs, and fill the frame with them.

Colour

Pick out objects that have striking colours. Try to limit the number of colours in the picture, or maybe even photograph a single colour.

Answers

Brain-teasers (page 16)

Many months
October does not appear in the word search.

Birthday girls
Debi was born in 1996 (a leap year).
Keisha was born in 1995.
Kerry was born in 1997.

Lost property

Check your calendars

Different diaries
A and F are the same.

All ages
Emma was born in 1993.
Melissa was born in 1994.
Aimee was born in 1995.
Joanne was born in 1996.
Ashleigh was born in 1997.

Testing time (page 26)

Whether something will sink or float does not depend on its size or weight, but its *density*. An object with high density is *heavy for its size* – for example a stone has higher density than a piece of wood. A large metal ship is heavy but not very dense, so it floats.

Puzzle planet (page 32)

Spaced out
Neil is attached to spaceship A. Buzz is attached to B. Helen is attached to C.

Stars in your eyes
There are 35 stars in the galaxy.

Across the universe
Hannah is going to Jupiter.
Dawn is going to Pluto.
Banu is going to Saturn.
Michelle is going to Mars.

Missing meteor
Piece A finishes the jigsaw.

Comet's tale
All these planets are in the comet's tail: Saturn, Mars, Earth, Mercury, Neptune, Jupiter, Pluto, Uranus, Venus.

Star-crossed

Mind-bogglers (page 50)

Warm words
The word is TEMPERATURE.

Penguin puzzler

Get the hump

Muffler muddle
The scarves should be picked up in order B, E, C, A, D.

Cool countries?
Canada, Mexico
Greenland, India
Brazil, Sweden
Iceland, Egypt
Norway, Kenya

Hot spots
Leopards 6 and 7 are the same.

Brownie twisters (page 68)

Knotty problem
Ball A belongs to Ann.
B belongs to Jenny.
C belongs to Jo.

Flag break
Piece D finishes the puzzle.

Word search

Scrambled Sixes
Bwbachod
Gnome
Sprite
Imp
Pixie
Leprechaun
Kelpie
Ghillie-Dhu

To the point
Compass E has all the points in the right place.

Double trouble
The old name for Brownies is ROSEBUD.

Mixed signals
Becky and Olivia are signalling the same letter.

Run for it!

Get into the Olympic spirit! Have a go at this fun game with your friends, and find out who is the greatest marathon runner!

You need
❀ A die
❀ Counters

How to play
Throw the die and follow the instructions to move around the board. First to the finish line wins a gold medal!

START ★

1
2
Crowds cheer you! Go on 2
4
5
Trip over your feet Miss a go!
7
8
Run with your team mate Go on 1
10
11
Road goes uphill Go back 2
13
14

Illustrated by Stuart Lynch